A LifeGuide®

ECCLESIASTES

Chasing
After Meaning

12 studies
for individuals or groups

Bill &
Teresa Syrios

With Notes for Leaders

InterVarsity Press
Downers Grove, Illinois

To our sons Luke, Andrew, Phillip and Mark
When you notice this dedication . . . likely some years from now,
May you be reminded of your mom and dad's love for you and that:

In the pursuit of meaning you will find Jesus
And in the pursuit of Jesus you will find meaning.

It has been our greatest desire to pass on to you such a legacy.

InterVarsity Press
P.O. Box 1400, Downers Grove, IL 60515-1426
World Wide Web: www.ivpress.com
E-mail: mail@ivpress.com
©1992, 2002 by Bill and Teresa Syrios

InterVarsity Press® is the book-publishing division of InterVarsity Christian Fellowship/USA®, a student movement active on campus at hundreds of universities, colleges and schools of nursing in the United States of America, and a member movement of the International Fellowship of Evangelical Students. For information about local and regional activities, write Public Relations Dept., InterVarsity Christian Fellowship/USA, 6400 Schroeder Rd., P.O. Box 7895, Madison, WI 53707-7895, or visit the IVCF website at <www.ivcf.org>.

All Scripture quotations, unless otherwise indicated, are taken from the Holy Bible, New International Version®. NIV®. *Copyright ©1973, 1978, 1984 by International Bible Society. Used by permission of Zondervan Publishing House. All rights reserved.*

Cover photograph: Dennis Flaherty Photography

ISBN 0-8308-3027-8

Printed in the United States of America ∞

| P | 17 | 16 | 15 | 14 | 13 | 12 | 11 | 10 | 9 | 8 | 7 | 6 | 5 | 4 | 3 |
| Y | 16 | 15 | 14 | 13 | 12 | 11 | 10 | 09 | 08 | 07 | 06 | 05 | 04 | 03 |

Contents

Getting the Most Out of
Ecclesiastes

"Everything has changed." The words hung in her office like heavy drapes as I sat down for a meeting with Nancy, a very successful sales manager. And indeed, everything had. Today Nancy wanted to reflect on a most unusual topic for a business meeting: what is the meaning of life? Normally the epitome of efficiency, Nancy continued until every question got some kind of answer. I realized she was having an "Ecclesiastes moment." We both were.

The date was Friday, September 14, 2001, three days and four airplanes after everything changed. We were all asking these questions: Can anyone explain it? How could it make any real sense? Does anything make sense?

Teresa and I were in the middle of revising this LifeGuide Bible Study, and I happened to have a copy of the original version with me. As I handed it to Nancy, I said, "This guide was written about a book that takes on life's most difficult questions. As a matter of fact the very first sentence lays out the author's stunning conclusion, 'Meaningless! Meaningless! Everything is meaningless.'"

As Nancy and I continued to agonize aloud about life's meaning, I took the opportunity to introduce her to what I'm about to introduce to you—the one book in the Bible that just does *not* seem to fit. What place could such a harsh assertion of meaninglessness have in a Scripture that intends to reveal the redeeming work of God in history?

Along with the book of Job, Ecclesiastes reminds us that God is bigger, and our life in this world more unpredictable, than we might think. The book invites us to take a realistic tour of life. The sightseeing stops will likely leave those who enjoy nice, tidy answers rather perplexed, if not downright frustrated.

Who's the Author?

Our guide for this adventure is introduced by the Hebrew title: *qoheleth*. The title, which translated into Greek is *ekklesiastes*, comes from a Hebrew word for assembling. It suggests a type of office-bearer. Thus we have such translations as "the Preacher" (KJV, RSV, NASB), "the Speaker" (NEB), "the Philosopher" (TEV) and the one we will use in this guide, "the Teacher" (NIV).

The Teacher identifies himself as "son of David, king in Jerusalem" (1:1). Such an identification naturally links him with the wisest of all Israel's sages, King Solomon. Many commentators, however, believe that the Teacher was not actually Solomon but wrote in the tradition and from the perspective of Solomon.

The depth of insight found in the book would certainly argue for an author endowed with the kind of wisdom God granted to Solomon (see 1 Kings 3:5-12). If the Teacher was not actually King Solomon, he surely qualified as a star disciple of this master sage.

As a wise man, the Teacher represented a group whose influence and prestige grew to virtual equality with Israel's prophets and priests. Israel's wise men closely observed the interworking of nature and human experience. From this storehouse of wisdom, they made general pronouncements concerning life's most perplexing issues and counseled people who faced difficult decisions.

The three most notable works of Israel's wise men include Ecclesiastes, Job and Proverbs. Their mark on Old Testament literature may also be seen in the Song of Solomon, Lamentations and a number of the psalms (such as, 1, 37, 49, 73, 127, 133). This body of writing, called wisdom literature, has a strong influence on portions of the New Testament. Jesus frequently quotes proverbs and uses wise sayings. Paul often talks about the wisdom of God (see 1 Corinthians 1:18—2:16 as an example). And the book of James provides counsel in a style similar to Old Testament wisdom literature.

What's the Point?

The Teacher's message seems particularly aimed at the secularists— those who seek to find life's meaning outside of a practical faith in God. With despairing perception, the author explores a grim reality he calls "life under the sun"—life outside of God's control and goodness. He addresses some of life's most sensitive questions: Does life really have meaning? Who is in control? What does it take to find satisfaction or even be content? How do we live wisely?

Much of the time God is left out of the discussion. But when he gets introduced, everything changes. "Life under the sun" becomes "life from the hand of God." Chasing after meaning transforms into the pursuit of God. The exploration of life's meaninglessness outside of knowing God thus becomes an invitation to know him. In its own unique way, Ecclesiastes ultimately introduces the One who "came that we might have life abundantly"—Jesus Christ himself.

Understandably, then, Ecclesiastes warrants special study by anyone in a formative period of life. Colleges would do well to set up a course for their freshmen and sophomores with Ecclesiastes as required reading. They could call it "Basic Living 101."

As I told Nancy on that September day after everything changed, you don't have to go through a world-altering event or a near-death experience to have an Ecclesiastes moment. All you really need to do is read Ecclesiastes itself, and it will either drown you in pessimism or bring you up for air within a God-centered worldview and hope.

In keeping with the book's approach, the guide opens each new chapter not with a statement but with a question. May the Lord use Ecclesiastes to help us live in hope—the hope that putting Jesus in the center of life provides.

For Further Reading

For a full discussion of Ecclesiastes's authorship, as well as other related issues, including background and date, see Michael Eaton, *Ecclesiastes*, Tyndale Old Testament Commentaries (Downers Grove, Ill.: InterVarsity Press, 1983), or Derek Kidner, *The Wisdom of Proverbs, Job and Ecclesiastes: An Introduction to Wisdom Literature* (Downers Grove, Ill.: InterVarsity Press, 1985). Two other helpful commentaries on Ecclesiastes are Derek Kidner, *The Message of Ecclesiastes* (Downers Grove, Ill.: InterVarsity Press, 1976), and T. M. Moore, *Ecclesiastes: Ancient Wisdom When All Else Fails* (Downers Grove, Ill.: InterVarsity Press, 2001).

Suggestions for Individual Study

1. As you begin each study, pray that God will speak to you through his Word.

2. Read the introduction to the study and respond to the personal reflection question or exercise. This is designed to help you focus on God and on the theme of the study.

3. Each study deals with a particular passage—so that you can delve into the author's meaning in that context. Read and reread the passage to be studied. The questions are written using the language of the New International Version, so you may wish to use that version of the Bible. The New Revised Standard Version is also recommended.

4. This is an inductive Bible study, designed to help you discover for yourself what Scripture is saying. The study includes three types of questions. *Observation* questions ask about the basic facts: who, what, when, where and how. *Interpretation* questions delve into the meaning of the passage. *Application* questions help you discover the implications of the text for growing in Christ. These three keys unlock the treasures of Scripture.

Write your answers to the questions in the spaces provided or in a personal journal. Writing can bring clarity and deeper understanding of yourself and of God's Word.

5. It might be good to have a Bible dictionary handy. Use it to look up any unfamiliar words, names or places.

6. Use the prayer suggestion to guide you in thanking God for what you have learned and to pray about the applications that have come to mind.

7. You may want to go on to the suggestion under "Now or Later," or you may want to use that idea for your next study.

Suggestions for Members of a Group Study

1. Come to the study prepared. Follow the suggestions for individual study mentioned above. You will find that careful preparation will greatly enrich your time spent in group discussion.

2. Be willing to participate in the discussion. The leader of your group will not be lecturing. Instead, he or she will be encouraging the members of the group to discuss what they have learned. The leader will be asking the questions that are found in this guide.

3. Stick to the topic being discussed. Your answers should be based on the verses which are the focus of the discussion and not on outside authorities such as commentaries or speakers. These studies focus on a particular passage of Scripture. Only rarely should you refer to other portions of the Bible. This allows for everyone to participate in in-depth study on equal ground.

4. Be sensitive to the other members of the group. Listen attentively when they describe what they have learned. You may be surprised by their insights! Each question assumes a variety of answers. Many questions do not have "right" answers, particularly questions that aim at meaning or application. Instead the questions push us to explore the passage more thoroughly.

When possible, link what you say to the comments of others. Also, be affirming whenever you can. This will encourage some of the more hesitant members of the group to participate.

5. Be careful not to dominate the discussion. We are sometimes so eager to express our thoughts that we leave too little opportunity for others to respond. By all means participate! But allow others to also.

6. Expect God to teach you through the passage being discussed and through the other members of the group. Pray that you will have an enjoyable and profitable time together, but also that as a result of the study you will find ways that you can take action individually and/or as a group.

7. Remember that anything said in the group is considered confidential and should not be discussed outside the group unless specific permission is given to do so.

8. If you are the group leader, you will find additional suggestions at the back of the guide.

1

Is It All Meaningless?

The water in the glass measures exactly at the halfway point. Now comes the classic test to determine whether you are a pessimist or an optimist: Do you consider the glass of water to be half empty or half full?

GROUP DISCUSSION. Fill a clear glass halfway with water and set it on a table in the middle of the group. Then discuss the question above.

PERSONAL REFLECTION. How does being a pessimist or optimist (or something in between) affect your relationship with God and others?

If you're a half-empty type, you will find Ecclesiastes's author, the Teacher, a fast friend. If you're more of an optimist, you may find it harder to relate to him. But either way, realize he is delivering pessimism with a purpose. In his introduction he answers a question before he even raises it. The question is, "Can meaning in life come outside of a God-centered universe?" The answer? Well, hang on for some of Scripture's most brutal language. *Read Ecclesiastes 1:1-11.*

1. How do you react to the theme (or thesis) of the book, which the Teacher states in verses 2-3?

2. How do examples of nature support his thesis that "all is meaningless" (vv. 5-7)?

3. According to verse 8, seeking new experiences will not bring lasting satisfaction. When have you found this to be true in your own life?

4. From verses 9-10, describe the Teacher's view of history. What does he communicate by expressing such a view?

5. What might the Teacher say to a person who believes that educating people will eventually solve humanity's problems?

6. How does human mortality (vv. 4, 11) bring the Teacher's argument to a climax?

7. Suppose you met the Teacher and got into a conversation. In what ways would you agree that "all is meaningless"?

In what ways do you sense that people around you live with a sense of despair?

8. As a Christian, on what basis would you seek to refute the Teacher's thesis?

9. What is an area of struggle in your life that has recently seemed futile or meaningless?

10. If there is nothing that brings meaning "under the sun," what resources from above—from God—can bring hope to your situation?

Ask God for a renewed sense of his vision for your life that transcends a pessimistic or optimistic nature.

Now or Later

Read *Ecclesiastes 1—6 (or to 12 if time allows)*. How does Ecclesiastes effectively communicate the gospel message?

How could you see using it to share Jesus with a family member, friend or coworker?

Consider asking one person who is not yet a follower of Jesus to read the first three chapters of Ecclesiastes and tell you what they think. If they're interested, invite them to study it with you!

2

Where Can We Find Fulfillment?

Imagine a total plunge into hedonism—following every possible avenue of self-seeking pleasure and satisfaction. Now let your imagination grow further, having the political and financial means to indulge yourself to the fullest possible extent . . . and with *no guilt!*

GROUP DISCUSSION. Pass out a number of magazines and look through the advertisements. What avenues do people look to today in their quest for fulfillment?

PERSONAL REFLECTION. If there is one thing, other than God, that you are tempted to give yourself to, what is it?

Hedonist imagination turns to reality in this section of Ecclesiastes—surely one of the most colorful passages in the Bible. Here is one person's attempt at something many only dream about. *Read Ecclesiastes 1:12-18.*

1. How does the Teacher describe himself and his quest?

2. Why does the author call his search for wisdom "a heavy burden" (1:13)?

_____

3. What does the Teacher conclude from his quest?

In what ways have you found this to be true?

_____

4. *Read Ecclesiastes 2:1-16.* Describe the various avenues the Teacher tested in his quest for fulfillment.

How does he expect to find fulfillment through these things?

_____

5. What advantages would he have over the average person in his search for satisfaction?

_____

6. How have you, with more limited resources, carried out a similar quest?

_____

7. In 2:12-16 he outlines two approaches to discovering meaning in life. What are the advantages and limitations of these two approaches?

---

8. What prompts his change of perspective (2:14-16)?

---

9. In the first six chapters the Teacher repeats his thesis that "all is meaningless" twenty-one times. How does he show that life is meaningless in 1:12—2:16?

---

10. How have you been convinced of the meaninglessness of living outside of Christ's lordship?

---

11. What would help you turn your desire for meaning in life into a wholehearted pursuit of God?

Pray that God would transform your "small ambitions" into his great ambition for you.

Now or Later

Meditate on Matthew 6:33: "Seek first his kingdom and his righteousness, and all these things will be given to you as well." How does this verse give perspective to your life right now?

3

What Is the
Value of Work?

Gary hates his job. The tasks are repetitive, his boss is a grouch, the other employees bicker. The job, however, pays better than anything else he could find. Gary feels trapped.

Nothing can be quite as frustrating as work. And while most of us can't fully identify with Gary, many of us can readily understand something about his predicament.

GROUP DISCUSSION. Whether you are working for pay right now or not, describe what you would consider your "job." What do you like most about it, and what do you like least about it?

PERSONAL REFLECTION. How has God provided for your financial needs throughout your life?

In this section of Ecclesiastes, the Teacher will look back at his own life's work. If anyone had a great job, he did. Even so, he asks, "Does it really amount to anything significant?" *Review Ecclesiastes 1:12—2:16.*

1. How would you describe the Teacher's quest for meaning up to this point?

2. *Read Ecclesiastes 2:17-26.* How would you describe the Teacher's emotional state as a result of his quest?

---

3. The phrase "under the sun" is used often throughout Ecclesiastes. It appears twice in this passage (vv. 17, 22). How would you describe the under-the-sun mentality?

---

4. What impact does the repetition of this phrase have on you?

---

5. Where do you find under-the-sun thinking around you?

---

6. What does the Teacher say about work in verses 21-23?

---

7. What would he say about workaholic tendencies in our society?

How could his perspective on work help with this mentality?

8. What shift do you see in the way the Teacher views work in verses 24-26?

9. Describe the contrast between seeking pleasure (vv. 10-11) and finding enjoyment (vv. 24-26).

10. When have you experienced the kind of satisfying enjoyment described here?

11. If you were to view your work as a gift from God to be enjoyed, how could that change your attitude about it?

Consider the attitude expressed in Colossians 3:23: "Whatever you do, work at it with all your heart, as working for the Lord, not for men." Pray for God's help as you seek to live this out.

Now or Later

Compare your vocation (calling) as a follower of Jesus and his ambassador (see 2 Corinthians 5:20) to your paid job (or your responsibility as a stay-at-home parent). How can your vocation bring greater purpose to your work endeavors?

4

Who Is Really in Control?

Ecclesiastes 3:1—4:3

"Why do the innocent suffer?" is a question that has plagued the conscience of humanity. And we also wonder, "Why do the unrighteous prosper?" Both of these questions can lead to despair, suggesting that life is indeed meaningless.

GROUP DISCUSSION. Which of the above questions bothers you most? Why do you think one bothers you more than the other?

PERSONAL REFLECTION. Think of an event of injustice you have personally experienced. What toll did it take on you?

This famous chapter of Ecclesiastes poses a solution for life's bothersome dilemma. The solution hinges on how we answer a third question: Who is really in control? If people are in charge, then life is a game of chance whose rules are controlled by the most powerful among us. But if a just and loving God is in charge, then eternity intersects our circumstances with a lifelong series of divine appointments. *Read Ecclesiastes 3:1—4:3.*

1. Describe the Teacher's view of time in verses 1-8.

2. How do you interpret this way of looking at time? (Is it despairing or hopeful—or both?) Explain.

3. What negative and positive things does the Teacher say about time in verses 9-15?

4. How would you live your life differently if you believed God had no control?

What consequences of not acknowledging God's authority are taking place in our society?

5. How does God's sovereign control of time and eternity bring meaning to life?

What difference would it make if you lived as if every person and circumstance that came your way was a "divine appointment"?

6. What observations does the Teacher make in 3:16 and 4:1-3 about human wickedness?

7. How do you struggle with the tension of knowing God is in control and yet seeing wickedness in control?

8. In the future God will bring judgment (3:17). For the present, however, God brings us a test (3:18-22). What is the test and its desired result?

9. Contrast the worldview of 3:18-22 with that of 3:11-15.

10. What kind of perspective results from evaluating wickedness from an earthly viewpoint (4:1-3)?

11. What kind of perspective results from evaluating wickedness from an eternal viewpoint (3:17)?

12. What is one area in which you need to exercise faith and confidence in God's sovereign control for the upcoming week?

Thank God for his loving and just oversight in a situation that you think is unfair or unjust. Pray for his intervention.

Now or Later

Think through the events of today (get out your scheduler, if helpful). Consider each person you are meeting with or activity you are involved in as if God is right there with you—he is! What difference will his presence make?

5

What Attitudes Should We Embrace?

Ecclesiastes 4:4—5:7

"The church is full of hypocrites!" Christians often hear this from those outside the church. Instead of uncomfortable acknowledgment of the obvious, I like to respond by saying, "Yes, but if you think they're bad now, you should have seen them before God got hold of them!"

GROUP DISCUSSION. On a piece of paper complete the following with a definition or illustration: A hypocrite is _____. Take a vote on the definition or illustration that you think is most helpful.

PERSONAL REFLECTION. Isn't the biggest hypocrite the person who will not acknowledge that he or she is, to some extent, a hypocrite? What is an area of your life that you would like to see line up more with your beliefs?

When it comes to how faith should change a person's life, expectations are high. And rightly so. We become like those we live around, and if that includes the Lord, then we will see our lives begin to reflect his. In this passage the Teacher explores some everyday values and attitudes that a relationship with God should influence. *Read Ecclesiastes 4:4-16.*

---

1. What are the negative consequences of the two extreme attitudes described in 4:4-5?

---

2. What irony concerning the workaholic's efforts is spoken about in 4:7-8?

---

3. On a scale of 1 to 10 (1 being lazy and 10 being a workaholic), how would you rate yourself? Explain.

How could the balance envisioned in 4:6 help you?

---

4. What are the benefits of partnership (4:9-12)?

---

5. Why is such an attitude critical in the Christian community?

6. In terms of your need for other people, are you primarily a dependent or independent person? Explain.

How does the Teacher's wisdom challenge you toward growth in interdependence with others?

---

7. Ecclesiastes 4:13-16 outlines a rags-to-riches story. What, however, is the ironic twist to its ending?

---

8. What examples in your experience illustrate the insecure nature of achieving prestige and power?

---

9. *Read Ecclesiastes 5:1-7.* Contrast the two approaches to God described in 5:1-7.

10. In 5:7 the Teacher exhorts his readers to "stand in awe of God." In what ways are you guilty of taking God too lightly?

---

11. We have thus far run across five negative attitudes—laziness, workaholism, unhealthy independence, foolish ambition and a lack of respect for God. If you could remove one negative attitude that you struggle with, which one would it be?

What could you do to replace that negative attitude with a positive one?

Thank God for his forgiveness. Ask him for renewed strength to be the person you and he wants you to be.

Now or Later

Skim Jesus' description of righteous living found in the Sermon on the Mount (Matthew 5—7). Spend time taking personal inventory and making confession.

6

What Does It Take to Be Content?

Ecclesiastes 5:8—6:12

If the advertisers are right, we have a lot to feel discontent about. We don't have enough possessions, and what we do have is not up-to-date enough. Fulfillment is equated with wearing the right kind of clothes, driving the right kind of car, drinking the right kind of beverage. How silly. How insidious.

GROUP DISCUSSION. Make two columns on a piece of paper entitled "My Needs" and "My Wants," and fill them out. What did you discover? What things do people in your age group feel least content about?

PERSONAL REFLECTION. Thank God for how he has met your needs and even many of your wants.

The same lifestyle of discontent that infects our culture also held sway for many of the Teacher's contemporaries. In this section he challenges his readers to stop seeking satisfaction from accumulating things. Instead he offers an alternative, one that leads to a lifestyle of contentment. *Read Ecclesiastes 5:8-20.*

---

1. How does the Teacher describe the nature of wealth?

2. What negative effects does the desire for wealth have in public life (5:8-9)?

in personal life (5:10-17)?

3. On a scale of 1 to 10 (1 being very little, 10 being very much), how would you rate your attachment to the things you own?

Describe one particular struggle you have had in this area.

4. How do your possessions relate to your sense of security?

5. *Read Ecclesiastes 6:1-12.* Note the contrast between 5:18-20 and 6:1-2. What role does God have in the satisfaction that wealth, possessions and honor can bring?

6. Give an example of how viewing possessions as a gift of God would help to change your attachment to them.

7. Many children and a long life were considered the greatest of blessings in the Old Testament (6:3-6). What does our society define as "the good life"?

_____

8. How do you understand Scripture to define "the good life"? (Also see the Beatitudes in Matthew 5:1-12.)

Do you find it difficult living a biblical version of "the good life" at times? Explain.

_____

9. In 6:7-12 the Teacher uses questions to challenge his readers. How would the questions challenge an unbeliever (see especially 6:12)?

_____

10. How could you exercise trust in God for an area in which you lack contentment?

Thank God for his abundant promises to you in this life and the one hereafter.

Now or Later

Focus in on Matthew 6:19-34. There are two commands for living a life of contentment—verses 19 and 25. How does Jesus explain the logic supporting the choice of such a lifestyle?

7

Where Can We Find Wisdom?

Ecclesiastes 7:1—8:1

Regret. Who among us does not at least occasionally succumb to the temptation to look back and question past decisions? And if we don't ever look back, most likely we should.

GROUP DISCUSSION. Squeeze some toothpaste onto a plate and see if anyone in the group can get the toothpaste back into the tube. How does this exercise illustrate how hard it is to take back our words or actions once they're said or done?

PERSONAL REFLECTION. What are some of the decisions you most regret?

What consequences do you live with now?

Sometimes inadequate information hinders us from making good decisions. But often we simply lack the necessary wisdom to make the right choice at the right time. In this section the Teacher will address where such wisdom comes from and how we can capitalize on it for future decisions. *Read Ecclesiastes 7:1—8:1.*

1. What are ways the Teacher describes wisdom?

What is the difference between knowledge and wisdom?

—————————————————————————————————————

2. Are you surprised by any of the comparisons in 7:1-6? Explain.

—————————————————————————————————————

3. How can suffering and sorrow offer instruction for living?

—————————————————————————————————————

4. Describe how a painful experience produced a positive change in your own life.

—————————————————————————————————————

5. What dangers does the Teacher warn against in verses 7-10?

—————————————————————————————————————

6. Do you agree with the description of wisdom in verses 11-12? Explain.

What are the limits of human wisdom according to verses 13-15?

—————————————————————————————————————

7. Have you ever been frustrated that God didn't intervene to change a difficult situation? Explain.

—————————————————————————————————————

8. Why does he give the warning of verses 16-18 in the terms he uses?

9. Describe how fearing God puts life into perspective (v. 18).

10. What perspective does wisdom provide according to verses 19-22?

11. What further observations does the Teacher make from his quest for wisdom (7:23—8:1)?

12. From this section of Ecclesiastes, Chuck Swindoll defines *wisdom* as "the God-given ability to see life with rare objectivity and to handle life with rare stability."* In what areas of your Christian life do you presently need such objectivity and stability?

Pray for God's wisdom in an upcoming decision (see James 1:5).

Now or Later

Read 1 Kings 3. In verse 5 God grants Solomon a wish, and Solomon asks for wisdom (v. 9). Why is God so pleased with Solomon's response, and how does he bless him for it?

---

*Charles Swindoll, *Living on the Ragged Edge Bible Study Guide* (Fullerton, Calif.: Insights for Living, 1986), p. 74.

8

How Shall We Live
Under Authority?

Ecclesiastes 8:2-17

Does your foot automatically come off the accelerator pedal when you buzz by a police car on the side of the road? Do your eyes then anxiously glance up to the rearview mirror? Sure we respect authority—when we have to. But can living under authority enrich our lives?

GROUP DISCUSSION. Think up as many symbols of authority as you can (for example, police badge, Do Not Enter sign, salute and so on). Which ones do you sense yourself reacting to positively, and which ones do you react to negatively? Why?

PERSONAL REFLECTION. If you could ask God one question about how the circumstances of your life have gone, what would it be and why?

In this study the Teacher outlines some positive benefits of relating to both human and divine authority. *Read Ecclesiastes 8:2-17.*

1. Why does the Teacher encourage obedience to authority?

2. What is significant about the fact that human authority is limited (v. 8)?

_____

3. Think of one life setting in which you relate to authority (for example, family, job, school or church). What is your biggest struggle in living under this authority?

How has this source of authority brought positive benefits to your life?

_____

4. Now choose a life setting in which you exercise authority. What is your biggest struggle in wisely exercising authority in this situation?

_____

5. What unjust uses of authority are described (vv. 9-11, 14)?

_____

6. How would you characterize the Teacher's answer to these injustices in verses 12-13?

_____

7. How does God's authority, alluded to in verses 15-17, contrast with human limitations in verses 7-8?

8. How is allowing God to have authority in our lives more beneficial than operating under our own sense of authority?

9. In the face of life's injustices and uncertainties, the Teacher argues for enjoying life (v. 15). Why?

10. According to verses 16-17, human wisdom is very limited. How should knowing this fact encourage fearing and trusting God?

11. What is an unsettled situation in life that you need to entrust to God?

Pray for those in authority: political leaders as well as your pastor, campus and church leaders. Pray also for areas and people you exercise some kind of authority over.

Now or Later

Proverbs 9:10 says, "The fear of the LORD is the beginning of wisdom." How would you relate fearing the Lord to appropriately responding to his authority?

How does this verse relate to your situation?

9

What Meaning Does Death Bring to Life?

On the edge of the University of Oregon campus lies a sizable historical cemetery. For many students the cemetery represents an unfortunate obstacle as they crisscross the campus from one class to the next. But I doubt the Teacher would share this objection. What better reminder for young people seeking to fashion lifelong values? Contemplation of death gives us the wisdom to live.

GROUP DISCUSSION. Have each person alternately lie on a couch or the floor. It's your funeral. The group gathers to say some words about what your life has meant to them. But instead of the group saying nice things about you, you say what you'd like to hear—what you'd like to be known for.

PERSONAL REFLECTION. What difference would it make in your life if you knew you were going to die within six months?

Read Ecclesiastes 9:1-12.

1. In what ways are the righteous and wicked described in verses 1-3?

2. What reaction might the Teacher hope to gain with his emphasis that a "common destiny" awaits all (vv. 1-3)?

3. Why do most people have a hard time coming to grips with death?

4. Do you feel uneasy about your own eventual death? Explain.

5. What kind of hope does the Teacher offer in verses 4-6?

6. How can a proper perspective toward death affect your priorities and values in life?

Look at the group discussion question. Are you living in such a way that ensures these things will be said at your funeral?

7. In what ways do verses 7-10 encourage us to enjoy life?

8. How can you enjoy life in the face of death?

9. What uncertainty do the factors of time and chance bring to life (vv. 11-12)?

10. How does the reality of death help you put your particular struggles into perspective?

11. How do Christ's death and resurrection give you hope in this life and the one to come?

Thank God for the hope that Jesus' death and resurrection bring to you.

Now or Later

Read John 11:1-44. How does Jesus relate to Mary's and Martha's grief?

What is the significance of his words in verse 25—"I am the resurrection and the life"—for you? (See also Paul's perspective on Jesus' resurrection in 1 Corinthians 15:12-28.)

10

How Do We Live Sensibly?

Common sense. Do you sometimes feel that you missed out on this body of wisdom that is supposedly so universal, so common?

GROUP DISCUSSION. Think of as many commonsense sayings as you can ("a penny saved is a penny earned," "what goes up must come down" and so on). Then try making a few modern proverbs of your own.

PERSONAL REFLECTION. What is an area of life in which you sometimes feel out of control when it comes to applying commonsense wisdom?

We all lack commonsense judgment at times. But in this section the Teacher addresses something deeper and darker, the lack of a commonsense lifestyle. Such a lifestyle—called foolishness—results when human weakness and wickedness assert control. In this study the teacher will identify foolish behavior and tell us how to avoid it. *Read Ecclesiastes 9:13—10:20.*

1. Describe the ironies of wisdom and foolish behavior illustrated in 9:13-16.

---

2. What lessons can we learn from this example?

---

3. In reference to 9:17-18, do you find yourself giving more respect to those who have wisdom or to those who have status? Why?

---

4. How have you seen wisdom destroyed in a manner described in 9:18—10:1?

---

5. What is the significance of folly's description in 10:2-3?

---

6. What ironic situations are described in 10:5-7?

---

7. List the common situations described in 10:8-11 that call for the exercise of good judgment.

8. What is an area of life in which you struggle to exercise good judgment? Explain.

At what times are you most likely to make a poor judgment?

9. How can words betray a fool (10:12-14)?

10. What are the consequences of wise and foolish lifestyles according to 10:16-20?

11. James 1:5 says, "If any of you lacks wisdom, he should ask God, who gives generously." What is an area of your life that currently requires godly attitudes or action?

Ask God for the kind of wisdom that leads to godliness.

Now or Later

Skim through Proverbs (note there are thirty-one chapters). Pick out a few wise sayings that are meaningful for you right now. Consider taking the next month to read through one chapter of Proverbs per day. Write out a "proverb for the day" that is particularly helpful.

11

Is It Worth the Risk?

All week I prepared myself mentally and physically to rappel off Inspiration II, a sheer cliff of 100 feet near Bear Trap Ranch in Colorado. For me Inspiration II represented a test of resolve. The day that I was to go came, but I was busy with a camping trip. The next day no one was going. The day after that something else came up. From then until the end of the week I was going to make the rappelling trip . . . tomorrow. It never happened. To this day, thirty years later, I wonder, *Why didn't I go? Was I unsure of my skills, was I too timid to take up the challenge?*

GROUP DISCUSSION. Each group member has been given $100,000 and a die with the opportunity of increasing your amount by choosing a number from one to six. If you're right, you receive $1,000,000. If you're wrong, you lose your $100,000. (One in six equals a 16.67 percent chance of winning for a potential gain of 1,000 percent.) Are you willing to roll the die or not? Explain your choice.

What would be the lowest gain that would be worth you taking a roll of the die, if at all?

PERSONAL REFLECTION. What's something you've done which involved a great deal of risk?

There is a risk to not taking risks. An opportunity for gain in testing our resolve or pursuing a challenge may be lost forever. Failing to take spiritual risks in the life of faith has even greater consequences. In this section the Teacher will encourage us to exercise our faith by "casting our bread upon the waters." *Read Ecclesiastes 11.*

---

1. What is the Teacher encouraging in verses 1-6?

---

2. Given what the Teacher has said in chapters 1—10, why would he encourage us to be risk takers?

---

3. What does taking risks in our spiritual lives do for our relationship with God?

---

4. What risk-taking effort have you made recently, and what were the positive or negative results?

---

5. Describe the perspective on life found in verses 7-10.

---

6. On a scale of 1 to 10 (1 being very little and 10 being very much) how would rate your ability to enjoy life? Explain.

---

7. How does the perspective of verses 7-10 encourage you to pursue joy?

8. *Read Ecclesiastes 12:1-8.* What kind of relationship with God does the word *remember* imply (12:1, 6)?

———————————————————————————————

9. How do the metaphors in 12:2-5 describe the deterioration brought about in old age?

———————————————————————————————

10. Why should such deterioration encourage commitment to the Lord during our youth (12:1)?

———————————————————————————————

11. What are the metaphors used to describe death (12:6-7)?

———————————————————————————————

12. Why should the eventuality of death be a strong encouragement to a risk-taking commitment to God?

Spend several minutes thanking the Lord for the life that you have found in him.

Now or Later

During the communion of the Last Supper, Jesus instructed his disciples to "do this in remembrance of me" (Luke 22:19). Write down the word *remember* in a few strategic locations around your home or work environment. When people ask you why you've written that word around, tell them about Ecclesiastes.

What events (like Communion), places or anniversaries help you remember God and his goodness to you? Praise him for those memories.

12

What Makes Life Meaningful?

Ecclesiastes 12:9-14

If you were given the assignment to describe life with one word, what word would you choose? Few of us are comfortable with the Teacher's choice of *meaningless*.

GROUP DISCUSSION. On a piece of paper, sum up the message of Ecclesiastes in a brief phrase or statement. Take a group vote on which summation you like the best.

PERSONAL REFLECTION. What lesson from Ecclesiastes have you found the most compelling?

The phrase "all is meaningless" gets our attention—exactly what the Teacher intended. In utter darkness, a few small lights will stand out. These lights from Ecclesiastes—the purposes, values and priorities that should guide our lives—are now seen so much more clearly. Let's take one last look at how to pursue meaning in life, Ecclesiastes style.

1. How would you characterize the Teacher's pursuit to find meaning in life? (See 1:12—6:12.)

2. How does 2:24-26 act as a turning point in his argument?

3. Characterize the Teacher's priorities in life (see 11:1—12:8).

4. What is one way the Teacher's perspective on life has been helpful to you?

5. *Read Ecclesiastes 12:9-14.* How is the Teacher's purpose described in verses 9-10?

6. How do you think the Teacher would encourage caution as people pursue wisdom today?

7. Why is it significant that the Teacher's words are based on the authority of the "one Shepherd" (v. 11)?

8. Describe how seeking the Shepherd's wisdom is different from seeking other sources of wisdom.

9. Why do you think the Teacher ends his book with the particular directives of verses 13-14?

10. What does it mean for you to "fear God and keep his commandments" (v. 13)?

11. In light of your study of Ecclesiastes, on what basis is life meaningless to you, and on what basis is it not?

12. In what ways would you like to see your life affected by the message of Ecclesiastes?

Pray for renewed spiritual strength to live out your commitment to the Lord.

Now or Later

In Jesus we find meaning, reality, wisdom—summed up by the word *life* (review John 1:4; 6:35; 10:10; 11:25 and 14:6). Look at the questions raised by the titles for each study (see the table of contents). How does God's gift in Jesus answer those questions for you?

What, in a sentence or paragraph, is your understanding of the meaning of life?

Leader's Notes

MY GRACE IS SUFFICIENT FOR YOU. (2 COR 12:9)

Leading a Bible discussion can be an enjoyable and rewarding experience. But it can also be *scary*—especially if you've never done it before. If this is your feeling, you're in good company. When God asked Moses to lead the Israelites out of Egypt, he replied, "O Lord, please send someone else to do it"! (Ex 4:13). It was the same with Solomon, Jeremiah and Timothy, but God helped these people in spite of their weaknesses, and he will help you as well.

You don't need to be an expert on the Bible or a trained teacher to lead a Bible discussion. The idea behind these inductive studies is that the leader guides group members to discover for themselves what the Bible has to say. This method of learning will allow group members to remember much more of what is said than a lecture would.

These studies are designed to be led easily. As a matter of fact, the flow of questions through the passage from observation to interpretation to application is so natural that you may feel that the studies lead themselves. This study guide is also flexible. You can use it with a variety of groups—student, professional, neighborhood or church groups. Each study takes forty-five to sixty minutes in a group setting.

There are some important facts to know about group dynamics and encouraging discussion. The suggestions listed below should enable you to effectively and enjoyably fulfill your role as leader.

Preparing for the Study

1. Ask God to help you understand and apply the passage in your own life. Unless this happens, you will not be prepared to lead others. Pray too for the various members of the group. Ask God to open your hearts to the message of his Word and motivate you to action.

2. Read the introduction to the entire guide to get an overview of the

entire book and the issues which will be explored.

3. As you begin each study, read and reread the assigned Bible passage to familiarize yourself with it.

4. This study guide is based on the New International Version of the Bible. It will help you and the group if you use this translation as the basis for your study and discussion.

5. Carefully work through each question in the study. Spend time in meditation and reflection as you consider how to respond.

6. Write your thoughts and responses in the space provided in the study guide. This will help you to express your understanding of the passage clearly.

7. It might help to have a Bible dictionary handy. Use it to look up any unfamiliar words, names or places. (For additional help on how to study a passage, see chapter five of *Leading Bible Discussions,* InterVarsity Press.)

8. Consider how you can apply the Scripture to your life. Remember that the group will follow your lead in responding to the studies. They will not go any deeper than you do.

9. Once you have finished your own study of the passage, familiarize yourself with the leader's notes for the study you are leading. These are designed to help you in several ways. First, they tell you the purpose the study guide author had in mind when writing the study. Take time to think through how the study questions work together to accomplish that purpose. Second, the notes provide you with additional background information or suggestions on group dynamics for various questions. This information can be useful when people have difficulty understanding or answering a question. Third, the leader's notes can alert you to potential problems you may encounter during the study.

10. If you wish to remind yourself of anything mentioned in the leader's notes, make a note to yourself below that question in the study.

Leading the Study

1. Begin the study on time. Open with prayer, asking God to help the group to understand and apply the passage.

2. Be sure that everyone in your group has a study guide. Encourage the group to prepare beforehand for each discussion by reading the introduction to the guide and by working through the questions in the study.

3. At the beginning of your first time together, explain that these studies are meant to be discussions, not lectures. Encourage the members of the group to participate. However, do not put pressure on those who may be hes-

itant to speak during the first few sessions. You may want to suggest the following guidelines to your group.

☐ Stick to the topic being discussed.

☐ Your responses should be based on the verses which are the focus of the discussion and not on outside authorities such as commentaries or speakers.

☐ These studies focus on a particular passage of Scripture. Only rarely should you refer to other portions of the Bible. This allows for everyone to participate in in-depth study on equal ground.

☐ Anything said in the group is considered confidential and will not be discussed outside the group unless specific permission is given to do so.

☐ We will listen attentively to each other and provide time for each person present to talk.

☐ We will pray for each other.

4. Have a group member read the introduction at the beginning of the discussion.

5. Every session begins with a group discussion question. The question or activity is meant to be used before the passage is read. The question introduces the theme of the study and encourages group members to begin to open up. Encourage as many members as possible to participate, and be ready to get the discussion going with your own response.

This section is designed to reveal where our thoughts or feelings need to be transformed by Scripture. That is why it is especially important not to read the passage before the discussion question is asked. The passage will tend to color the honest reactions people would otherwise give because they are, of course, supposed to think the way the Bible does.

You may want to supplement the group discussion question with an icebreaker to help people to get comfortable. See the community section of *Small Group Idea Book* for more ideas.

You also might want to use the personal reflection question with your group. Either allow a time of silence for people to respond individually or discuss it together.

6. Have a group member (or members if the passage is long) read aloud the passage to be studied. Then give people several minutes to read the passage again silently so that they can take it all in.

7. Question 1 will generally be an overview question designed to briefly survey the passage. Encourage the group to look at the whole passage, but try to avoid getting sidetracked by questions or issues that will be addressed later in the study.

8. As you ask the questions, keep in mind that they are designed to be used just as they are written. You may simply read them aloud. Or you may prefer to express them in your own words.

There may be times when it is appropriate to deviate from the study guide. For example, a question may have already been answered. If so, move on to the next question. Or someone may raise an important question not covered in the guide. Take time to discuss it, but try to keep the group from going off on tangents.

9. Avoid answering your own questions. If necessary, repeat or rephrase them until they are clearly understood. Or point out something you read in the leader's notes to clarify the context or meaning. An eager group quickly becomes passive and silent if they think the leader will do most of the talking.

10. Don't be afraid of silence. People may need time to think about the question before formulating their answers.

11. Don't be content with just one answer. Ask, "What do the rest of you think?" or "Anything else?" until several people have given answers to the question.

12. Acknowledge all contributions. Try to be affirming whenever possible. Never reject an answer. If it is clearly off-base, ask, "Which verse led you to that conclusion?" or again, "What do the rest of you think?"

13. Don't expect every answer to be addressed to you, even though this will probably happen at first. As group members become more at ease, they will begin to truly interact with each other. This is one sign of healthy discussion.

14. Don't be afraid of controversy. It can be very stimulating. If you don't resolve an issue completely, don't be frustrated. Move on and keep it in mind for later. A subsequent study may solve the problem.

15. Periodically summarize what the group has said about the passage. This helps to draw together the various ideas mentioned and gives continuity to the study. But don't preach.

16. At the end of the Bible discussion you may want to allow group members a time of quiet to work on an idea under "Now or Later." Then discuss what you experienced. Or you may want to encourage group members to work on these ideas between meetings. Give an opportunity during the session for people to talk about what they are learning.

17. Conclude your time together with conversational prayer, adapting the prayer suggestion at the end of the study to your group. Ask for God's help in following through on the commitments you've made.

18. End on time.

Many more suggestions and helps are found in *Leading Bible Discussions*, which is part of the LifeGuide Bible Study series.

Components of Small Groups

A healthy small group should do more than study the Bible. There are four components to consider as you structure your time together.

Nurture. Small groups help us to grow in our knowledge and love of God. Bible study is the key to making this happen and is the foundation of your small group.

Community. Small groups are a great place to develop deep friendships with other Christians. Allow time for informal interaction before and after each study. Plan activities and games that will help you get to know each other. Spend time having fun together—going on a picnic or cooking dinner together.

Worship and prayer. Your study will be enhanced by spending time praising God together in prayer or song. Pray for each other's needs—and keep track of how God is answering prayer in your group. Ask God to help you to apply what you are learning in your study.

Outreach. Reaching out to others can be a practical way of applying what you are learning, and it will keep your group from becoming self-focused. Host a series of evangelistic discussions for your friends or neighbors. Clean up the yard of an elderly friend. Serve at a soup kitchen together, or spend a day working on a Habitat house.

Many more suggestions and helps in each of these areas are found in *Small Group Idea Book*. Information on building a small group can be found in *Small Group Leaders' Handbook* and *The Big Book on Small Groups* (both from InterVarsity Press). Reading through one of these books would be worth your time.

Study by Study Notes

General note. Jesus' Sermon on the Mount is to the New Testament what the Teacher's "sermon" is to the Old Testament. One may start off just a bit negatively—"All is meaningless"—and the other, rather positively: "Blessed are the poor in spirit." But while the approaches differ, the message is similar: Meaning in life—blessedness in life—comes from God-centered faith and faithfulness.

Of course, Jesus is the master of master sages, and the Teacher's efforts are but a foreshadowing of his astounding wisdom. So in your study of Ecclesiastes you may find it helpful to read and reread the Sermon on the Mount in Matthew 5—7 along the way. We refer to it in a number of the "Now or Later" questions.

Study 1. Ecclesiastes 1:1-11. Is It All Meaningless?

Purpose: To wrestle with the author's basic assertion that "all is meaningless."

Background note. Familiarize yourself with the introduction to Ecclesiastes at the front of the guide. It is particularly important to understand the perspective of the Teacher. He is a strong believer who knows that meaning in life comes only from a relationship with God. This realization becomes increasingly clear as the message of Ecclesiastes unfolds. Being a seasoned communicator, the Teacher does not spell out this perspective at the outset. Instead, he begins in the most negative of terms to grab his readers' attention, and grab it he does.

The introduction of Ecclesiastes (1:1-11) states the problem boldly: Taken at face value, life is meaningless. In introducing the book to your group, do not take away the "punch" of the Teacher's message by explaining away his negativism. Instead, let them deal with the totally bleak picture presented. Wait until question 8 to help them take on the Teacher from an alternate perspective.

Group discussion. This activity is meant to get people to recognize their own basic approach to life. Such an exercise will help them begin to identify with the Teacher and how he looks at life. Feel free to ask for illustrations to back up their answers in order to add color to the discussion (for example, "How does your optimism/pessimism come through in your friendships or the way you view money or your work?").

Question 1. It would be helpful to read all the different translations present for these verses. Verse 3 essentially puts the assertion in verse 2 in question form.

Question 3. This question is aimed at bringing out experiences we anticipated would bring great fulfillment—like buying something—but which ended up providing only a very temporary "fix" of satisfaction.

Question 4. Eastern religions hold to a circular view of history represented in such beliefs as reincarnation. But the Teacher's version is different: it's not that people go around (reincarnation) but that things go around. There is just nothing new under the sun. Sending a person to the moon or to Mars, for example, is not new in the sense of humanity's desire to explore frontiers. That desire has been with us since our beginning.

Question 6. The human mortality portrayed in verses 4 and 11 acts as bookends to the Teacher's argument. The fact that we are but blips on the radar screen of life lends the greatest weight to his thesis that indeed all is meaningless.

Question 7. You will probably have extra time at this point. Be prepared to lead your group into some in-depth sharing on this question and the ones that follow it. This will give group members a chance to get to know each other better.

Question 8. Here you can begin to challenge the Teacher's thesis with some God-centered realities (something he wants you to do!). For the Christian, the resurrection of Christ (see 1 Cor 15:12-28) gives hope and meaning to life. Also, Paul states that acts done out of faith, hope and love have eternal significance (1 Cor 13:13).

Questions 9-10. The Teacher wakes up his readers with the cold water of reality. Not a pleasant experience, but one with purpose. Instead of viewing him as a pessimist, it is more accurate to see him as a realist! The application here is meant to surface some of our own "treadmill experiences" and draw us to the Resource able to meet such frustrations.

Now or later. Ecclesiastes may very well be the most effective Old Testament book for introducing people to Jesus. Honest seekers will find themselves agreeing with the Teacher's hardcore realism. His perspective echoes the harsh reality Paul describes in Ephesians 2:12 of living "without God and without hope in this world." But the Teacher does not leave people hopeless because he knows when God takes the driver's seat, hope comes along for the ride!

Study 2. Ecclesiastes 1:12—2:16. Where Can We Find Fulfillment?

Purpose: To trace the Teacher's quest for fulfillment and grapple with his conclusions.

Group discussion. A follow-up question that would help the group get more specific is, "What avenues do your friends or coworkers explore in their quest for fulfillment?" Don't just dwell on the negative. There are both healthy and unhealthy avenues to find satisfaction.

Question 3. Note the implication of 1:16, the first potential answer given by the Teacher to the dilemma of life: what is needed is more wisdom.

Question 4. Note the implication in 2:1, the second potential answer to life's dilemma: what is needed are more experiences. Verse 11 summarizes the Teacher's findings that every avenue tested bore the fruit of futility.

Question 7. Note in 2:12 the Teacher's second look at his two proposals to give life meaning: "Wisdom is better than folly" (2:13), but alas, nothing works. Death ultimately makes a mockery of the Teacher's attempt to find meaning to life "under the sun."

Question 8. Verses 14-16 are a very humbling confession for a man who is an expert in the field of wisdom. Compare it to this example: The most valuable player in the Superbowl is interviewed on TV right after his team has won, and he tells the international listening audience that football has absolutely no significance in life.

Questions 10-11. Encourage group members to look hard at themselves and identify specific areas in which their convictions make no difference in how they live life. Here is where the message of Ecclesiastes will likely come home to people with spiritual sensitivity, for while we claim to believe in God, we often do not act as if we do. The great temptation is to live not as intellectual atheists but as practical atheists—orthodox in theology, heretical in practice!

Study 3. Ecclesiastes 2:17-26. What Is the Value of Work?

Purpose: To discover how a God-centered perspective on our work can make it a source of satisfaction and enjoyment.

Group discussion. This question offers an opportunity to get to know each other better. Encourage group members to describe what they do at their job, including homemakers and students.

Questions 1-2. Rereading Ecclesiastes 1:12—2:16 will help remind the group of the colorful description of the Teacher's quest. This will help dramatize the impact of his despair in 2:17-23. Wait to have the group read 2:24-26 until question 9 in order to emphasize its radical change of perspective.

Questions 3-5. The concept behind the phrase "under the sun" is critical to the message of the book. Life "under the sun" is life lived as if God does not exist. Today we call such a perspective secularism. And indeed, if we were going to label the Teacher, a term such as *antisecularist,* would be close to the mark.

Questions 6-7. The Teacher's thoughts about work are very personally expressed. Note all the personal pronouns in 2:17-20. His perspective, which gets universal expression in 2:21-23, offers a biting critique of workaholic tendencies. The work of managing creation was originally meant by God to give humanity great joy, and while much of this satisfaction survived the Fall, God's curse of the ground (Gen 3:17-19) forever added the element of "painful toil" to our work.

Question 8. Note the expression "from the hand of God" (v. 24). It would be helpful to explore how this expression acts as a contrast to the phrase "under the sun." The issue here is one of perspective. Only an eternal perspective that acknowledges spiritual realities can give meaning to our temporal existence.

Question 9. Chasing after fulfillment versus being content in all things are vastly different orientations. First help the group wrestle with the contrast between 2:10-11 and 2:24-26. Then guide the group into talking about how Christ makes the difference, but seek to avoid vague "Christian answers."

Questions 10-11. If you anticipate that your group will struggle in getting specific with applications, you may want to model what you're looking for by answering an application question yourself. Also, you can always respond to a vague answer with, "Can you give me a specific example of that?" (Remember this question and use it often!)

Study 4. Ecclesiastes 3:1—4:3. Who Is Really in Control?

Purpose: To explore the critical difference that a God-centered worldview makes in contrast to a secular worldview.

Group discussion. For a greater impact, start by referring to a couple of newspaper or magazine articles, one describing the suffering of an innocent person and another describing how a guilty person is not getting what he or she deserves.

Background note. The Teacher has been observing life through a microscope, concentrating his gaze downward. Now starting in 2:24, he exchanges his microscope for a telescope and adopts an entirely different perspective. Verses 1:12—2:23 illustrate the life of those living from the human perspective introduced in 1:2-11. In contrast, 3:1-15 illustrates the life of those living from the godly perspective introduced in 2:24-26. Thus 2:24—3:15 constitutes the Teacher's answer to life's apparent meaninglessness. In studying this section, we recommend that you first lead your group through study question 6 and then summarize the Teacher's argument in 1:1—3:15. This will help the group understand the author's overall reasoning.

Question 1. The Teacher uses the concept of time as a backdrop on which all human activity takes place. Beginning in verse 2 with birth and death, the author outlines fourteen polar opposites or two sets of seven couplets. Since seven represents completeness, the idea here is that these actions represent all human activity.

The well-known '60s song by the Byrds, "Turn, Turn, Turn," comes from Ecclesiastes 3:1-8. If you have access to it, play it for the group as an introduction.

Questions 2-3. Seen negatively, humanity is incapable of changing the cyclical nature of events. But seen positively, time has a God-ordained beauty (or appropriateness) to it. This contrasting perspective leads directly into question 3 concerning the conclusion of verses 9-15.

Question 4. Without a supreme authority, humanity becomes self-determining. Ethics degenerate into relativistic standards where the one in power sets the standards of right and wrong. Feel free to ask for examples in history to highlight this devastating situation as well as contemporary consequences in our own day and age.

Question 5. The issue of why a loving God allows evil may come up here. This is obviously a far-reaching question. It is clear that while God hates evil and cares about its tragic results in people's lives, he is still in control of what happens to us. The most evil act of all time—the crucifixion of the innocent Son of God—was done "by God's set purpose and foreknowledge" (Acts 2:23). His purpose in letting other acts of evil take their course may not be presently clear, but one day he will right every wrong (Rev 21:3-4), and all creation will praise him for the way he has chosen to run his universe (Phil 2:10-11).

After finishing question 5, you might want to take a couple of minutes to review with your group the structure of 1:1—3:15: (1) The problem stated (1:2): Life taken at face value is meaningless. (2) Potential solutions investigated: What is needed is more wisdom and knowledge (1:16). Critique: Wisdom and knowledge are meaningless (1:17-18). (3) What is needed are more experiences (2:1). Critique: Experience is meaningless (2:10-11). (4) Let's reconsider this desperate situation. Critique: Wisdom is better than folly, but nothing works (2:13-16). (5) Emotional response to these conclusions: anger and despair (2:17, 20). (6) Solution: What is needed is an entirely different worldview because to live under a secular worldview is meaningless (2:24—3:15). Starting in 2:24, God is mentioned three times in three verses. If God exists and is in control, as 3:1-15 goes on to assert, then living life based on this spiritual reality will fill existence with meaning and purpose. As one commentator puts it, "Secularism gives way to theism, pessimism to optimism, human autonomy to human faith."

Questions 6-7. Like other Hebrew thinkers, the Teacher's argument does not come in one large tidal wave of statements and supporting evidence. Instead, his thinking resembles waves crashing against the shore. He repeats his statements and evidence, each time developing his theme more fully. Consequently, in 3:16 and later in 4:1-3 the pervasive damage of human wickedness causes the author to again address the question of how God could really be in control.

Question 8. The Teacher's answer to the question of whether God is in control is that God is using this present life to test humanity. The first test is simply to see what life is like on a purely biological level. The test results come in that biologically humanity is both finite and fragile.

Help the group see the implications of this description. Humanity from a totally physical worldview is no more significant than your neighbor's obnoxious dog! Given our tentative biological nature, the Teacher implies the need for faith in a spiritual dimension.

Question 9. Just as verses 18-22 depict life on a purely physical level, verses 11-15 open the window to the light of spiritual reality.

Questions 10-11. Help the group see the parallel between the appropriate timing of human activity (3:1-8) as well as that of God's activity (3:17). God's judgment will assert its control over the one thing that might appear out of his control—human freedom. So even though injustice seems to now make a mockery of God's authority (4:1-3), at the appropriate time God's judgment will make a mockery of injustice.

Now or later. The idea that each and every person and event in our life comes about as a divine appointment amounts to a radical faith in God's sovereignty. Such a faith provides quite a contrast to "chasing after the wind."

Study 5. Ecclesiastes 4:4—5:7. What Attitudes Should We Embrace?

Purpose: To highlight a variety of negative and positive attitudes from which we can examine ourselves.

Group discussion. Your purpose here is not competition but illumination. To help the group not go overboard in describing "those people out there," you might ask for a personal illustration of hypocrisy (see the personal reflection question).

General note. Ecclesiastes 4:1—5:7 includes further observations the Teacher makes of people living on their own terms. Ironically, the Teacher is not talking to intellectual atheists (as 5:1-7 makes clear) but to religious people who are practical atheists. Whatever the short-term benefits of living the way one may deem best, it is better—and here is the key (4:9, 13; 5:5)—to live life based on God's values.

Questions 1-3. Ecclesiastes 4:4 describes one possible motive behind workaholic tendencies, namely, the craving to outshine or at least not to be outshone. There are, of course, other reasons behind overworking. Ecclesiastes 4:8 raises the question that should haunt all of us who have workaholic tendencies, no matter what the motive.

Questions 5-6. The term *interdependence* provides a balance between unhealthy dependence and individualistic independence. Most of us living in the affluent West, however, will probably need to examine our independent tendencies carefully.

Question 7. Ecclesiastes 4:13-16 portrays the short-lived acclaim of success. The old king should have the advantage of age but instead foolishly disregards advice. Then there is the poor but wise youth who startles everyone by his astounding climb to the top, but in reaching the top the youth ironically finds the same disrespect accorded to his predecessor.

Question 9. Religion becomes meaningless unless it is a heartfelt experience. Ecclesiastes 5:1-7 provides instruction for worshiping God with respect. A vow (5:4-5) in ancient Israel amounted to a promise to God. A broader definition would include living out our commitment to Christ as Lord of our lives.

Study 6. Ecclesiastes 5:8—6:12. What Does It Take to Be Content?
Purpose: To consider how viewing God as giver brings contentment in life.

Group discussion. Much of this section in Ecclesiastes speaks to the issue of one's wealth and possessions. But there are many other areas we lack contentment such as our physical appearance, relationships, work and lack of status. A good follow-up question here would be, "Which of the things mentioned are you least content about?"

Question 2. Things haven't changed. Money flows upward, toward power. The rich keep getting richer while the poor get poorer. Beyond this, as verses 5:10-17 indicate, an unhealthy desire for wealth leads to all kinds of personal damage.

Question 3. It would be helpful to go around the circle so each group member has an opportunity to share his or her rating and particular area of struggle asked for by this question. If people have trouble identifying a struggle in this area ask, "Do you ever feel tense about loaning something? Why do you think that is?"

Question 5. Note that the perspective of living life as a "gift of God" (5:19) is the polar opposite from living life under the sun.

Question 7. It may be helpful to have group members read a variety of translations for 6:3-6.

Question 8. Don't allow the group to give pat answers to the question. Use a follow-up question like "Can you give a specific example of that?" The second part of the question may create some soul-searching dialogue. If that happens, feel free to allow the group some time to discuss this important issue.

Question 9. By now you have noticed the intriguing way the Teacher argues his case. The questions in verses 6:7-12 epitomize his methodology: He argues for his viewpoint by pressing people to see what their viewpoint—a life-under-the-sun philosophy of life—leads to.

Ecclesiastes acts as an evangelistic appeal for those who are not yet Christians. The book should help genuine seekers ask the kind of questions that will lead them to the One who is "the way, the truth and the life." For Christians, an eternal perspective and security beyond the grave affects our ability to enjoy the present, in spite of our circumstances.

Question 10. You might want to refer back to the areas mentioned in the group discussion question as you ask this. Give group members some time to write out their answers. Then share them and pray together.

Study 7. Ecclesiastes 7:1—8:1. Where Can We Find Wisdom?
Purpose: To explore the sources, uses and limits of wisdom.

Group discussion. Supply toothpicks for those willing to try to get the toothpaste back in the tube.

Question 1. The contrast between knowledge (understanding facts) and wisdom (applying facts to life) should help sharpen your discussion about the unique qualities of wisdom. Another helpful contrast would involve advice (someone's opinion) and wisdom (which transcends personal opinion).

Question 2. Wisdom comes from the most unlikely places. For instance, it comes in the midst of what we may interpret as negative experiences—sorrow, mourning and death. Jesus expresses the Teacher's thoughts (vv. 3-4) in Matthew 5:3: "Blessed are the poor in spirit." Grief and brokenness over sin soften our hearts to God's remedy of forgiveness and cleansing in Christ. Realizing our spiritual poverty allows us to experience the vast riches of his joy.

Question 3. To make this question more concrete, follow it up with "Have you ever known of someone who has had a close brush with death? How did it change him or her?"

Question 4. This has the potential for producing some in-depth sharing. You might want to go around the circle, giving each person an opportunity to respond to it.

Question 8. The warning against being "overrighteous" (v. 16) probably refers to a self-righteous attitude, and "overwise" to a know-it-all attitude. In warning against being "overly wicked," the Teacher is not implying that a moderate amount of wickedness is acceptable! He simply recognizes the fact that wickedness is a part of human experience that needs to be controlled.

Question 10. Verses 21-22 contain the kind of self-evident wisdom that produces a smile as it cuts to the heart! Feel free to ask your group how they respond to it.

Question 11. Note in verse 26 that the Teacher is talking about a particular kind of woman. Any accusation that he is antiwomen misses the point, as we see from the contrasting picture of married love in 9:9. Moreover, the statement that wisdom is rare in men but rarer in women (v. 28) relates more to his experience than a sexist attitude. Real wisdom is seldom found in anyone. Since he has only found one wise man in a thousand, men who have wisdom outrate women by a margin of only one tenth of one percent! (Michael Eaton, *Ecclesiastes* [Downers Grove, Ill.: InterVarsity Press, 1983], p. 116.)

Question 12. As a creative exercise before answering this question, you could have your group write out and read their descriptions of wisdom along the lines of the description of love in 1 Corinthians 13. For example: Wisdom shows us our limitations and weaknesses. It develops humility in and vulnerability to God. Wisdom brings balance and wholeness to our relationships. It protects us from hasty decisions and protects others from our quick judgment. Wisdom shows us where our hope lies—in God alone.

Have each group member respond to question 12. If group members give vague answers ask, "Can you give us a specific illustration of that?" If needed, model such sharing by going first. After each person has answered, move into prayer for each group member. If appropriate, break the group down into twos or threes for the prayer time.

Study 8. Ecclesiastes 8:2-17. How Shall We Live Under Authority?

Purpose: To explore how we should live under the authority of God and others, and how to wisely exercise authority ourselves.

Group discussion. Come prepared with a list of symbols of authority and use them to prime the pump if your group members need some help thinking of these. Bring a poster-size piece of paper to write them down as group members verbalize them.

Question 1. Evidently it was a custom for the people to make an oath of loyalty to the king (v. 2). Leaving the king's presence (v. 3) could be considered an act of disloyalty, exposing oneself to retaliation.

Question 3. Be aware that the age of your group members and their situations in life will largely determine what authorities are present in their life.

Question 4. We all exercise authority over ourselves. Mention this if someone is having a difficult time coming up with a life setting in which they exercise authority.

Question 5. We have seen the role of human authority and its limitations. Now we are introduced to injustices in verses 9-11. All of this should encourage a faith in the limitless and positive authority of God (vv. 12-13).

Question 10. If we could completely figure out the ways of God, there would be little reason to fear him. We would be his peer. Instead, the more we acknowledge how little we understand, the more we will be spiritually in tune with him. "The fear of the LORD," as both the psalms and the proverbs assert, "is the beginning of wisdom" (Ps 111:10; Prov 9:10).

Study 9. Ecclesiastes 9:1-12. What Meaning Does Death Bring to Life?

Purpose: To consider how a proper perspective of death will lead to a proper perspective in life.

Group discussion. If you feel this exercise is not appropriate to your group, ask for volunteers or just describe it to them before asking the questions. But consider taking the risk of playing it out. It should add some helpful realism.

Question 2. Not only does it rain on the just and the unjust alike (Mt 5:45), death awaits both as well. Verses 1-3 act as a wake-up call to the reality of life's final event. There is no room for presumption in our relationship with God. Though their responses may differ, both the righteous and the wicked need to hear this message.

Questions 3-4. Depending on your group members' experience with loved ones dying or their own age and situation in life, these questions may bring up some strong feelings. Be prepared to direct people with sensitivity into what may be a difficult issue to face.

Question 5. These verses do not address the hope of eternal life. Instead they point to another kind of hope. A live dog (v. 4), despised in the ancient world as notoriously unclean, is better off simply because it is living than a dead lion, which was admired as a noble beast. While living, we still have part in what happens under the sun—opportunities for change and growth. Yet we know that we will die eventually, and because time is limited, we should evaluate what we do and set appropriate priorities.

Question 7. Do not miss the point that life is to be embraced and enjoyed. Such living in the face of death rests on the fact that we have God's favor (v. 7). White clothes and anointing oil (v. 8) were not to be shunned because they made life more enjoyable. Verse 10 acts as a summary. "Contentment (v. 7), comfort (v. 8) and companionship (v. 9) enable a man to throw himself into the tasks of life with energy and confidence" (Eaton, *Ecclesiastes*, p. 129).

Question 9. Two factors sidetrack the best-laid plans: time and chance. Lest we forget the lessons learned from death, we have constant reminders in unexpected and uncontrolled circumstances that mock our attempts to be self-sufficient. These disappointments, hurts and setbacks act as "mini-deaths," reminding us to place our dependence on God.

Question 11. This question gives the group an opportunity to broaden out the Teacher's perspective with that of the New Testament. The Teacher writes as if death is final and this life is all there is—and yet makes an argument for enjoying life. How much more would we enjoy life in the knowledge that death is not final!

Study 10. Ecclesiastes 9:13—10:20. How Do We Live Sensibly?

Purpose: To see how wisdom can guide one's life.

Group discussion. Think up a few of these so that if the group struggles you can help them, because "what goes around comes around." But don't boast about having such a great list, because "pride goes before a fall." And hey, if you think this is a pretty lousy way to get the point across, well all I can say is "those who live in a glass house shouldn't throw stones."

Question 1. Note the contrasts in this story: a small city and a few people versus a powerful king and huge siegeworks, and so on. The Teacher is most likely drawing on an actual incident to make his point. A good follow-up question would be "Have you known anyone like this wise man? Explain."

Question 2. Help the group relate the illustration of 9:13-16 to their own life and world. Our society's respect for the powerful and popular versus the wise and sensible can be readily seen in our own peer groups. We all need role models, particularly those who possess character qualities born from wisdom.

Question 4. This question is meant to give the group a "feel" for the proverb. It asks for an illustration from experience of how one person sidetracked a wise course of action.

Question 5. Note that foolishness here is portrayed as not just an isolated misjudgment but as a lifestyle of making poor judgments.

Question 6. In verse 10:6, "the rich" are identified in a positive way as those who have resources but lack opportunity to use them for the good of others.

Question 9. Verses 10:12-14 are the Old Testament equivalent of James 3:3-12. Words betray the inner condition of the heart, as mentioned earlier in Ecclesiastes 10:2. The issue of wisdom versus foolishness is not a matter of wise or stupid behavior but of morality and godliness versus wickedness.

Question 11. The need for wisdom is commonly linked to seeking guidance for decision making, but more appropriately, it should be linked to growth in Christlike behavior. God is not so much interested in where we are and what we're doing but in who we are and how we're doing. Help the group surface attitudes and actions they want to see transformed by godly wisdom.

Study 11. Ecclesiastes 11:1—12:8. Is It Worth the Risk?

Purpose: To consider how risk taking, joy and commitment to the Lord give meaning to life.

Group discussion. For this exercise go ahead and get out a die and see how each group member would have come out. Let the millionaires take the group out for ice cream after the meeting or bring it to the next one!

Questions 1-4. These questions are meant to focus on the need for taking risks in the life of faith. In the grim shadow of death (9:1-3) and of time and chance (9:11), it would be easy to become protective and self-seeking. But the Teacher encourages risk taking on the order of Jesus' words that "whoever loses his life for me and for the gospel will save it" (Mk 8:35). Boldness comes from facing the reality of life and death from the reality of God.

Questions 5-7. Help your group to feel the full force of the Teacher's admonition to pursue joy. In that pursuit the reminder of God's judgment (v. 9) protects us by putting the boundaries of morality around our pursuit of joy.

Question 8. This question should help people see that to "remember God" (12:1, 6) means much more than the mental act of thinking about him. Remembering connotes dropping any pretense that we are self-sufficient and committing ourselves unreservedly to the Lord. All the energy and passion of youth is certainly worth pouring into knowing him (Derek Kidner, *The Message of Ecclesiastes* [Downers Grove, Ill.: InterVarsity Press, 1976], p. 100).

Question 9. The metaphors of 12:2-5 are vivid but may not be fully appreciated. Impaired vision (vv. 2-3), control of the body (v. 3), loss of strength (v. 3) and hearing (v. 4) can understandably bring about fear of heights (v. 5) and the loss of desire (v. 5). "When the grinders cease" (v. 3) probably refers to losing teeth; "the almond tree blossoms" (v. 5) to hair turning gray or white; and "the grasshopper drags himself along" (v. 5) to the elderly person's slower movement (Swindoll, *Living on the Ragged Edge,* p. 120).

Study 12. Ecclesiastes 12:9-14. What Makes Life Meaningful?

Purpose: To consider how the purposes, values and priorities of Ecclesiastes should affect our life.

Group discussion. You might want to take the best effort, write it on a poster-size piece of paper, and hang it on the wall.

Questions 1-4. Allow group members enough time to skim the various sections, but do not allow the pace to drag. Ask people to give references when they share so others can follow along.

Question 6. Feel free to go around the circle with this question so that each group member has an opportunity to share.

Questions 7-8. The "one Shepherd" could be a designation for the king but is more likely a designation for God. In his best-known psalm, King David describes the Lord as his shepherd (Ps 23:1). Jesus promises the protection of "the Good Shepherd" to those who listen to the voice of the "one Shepherd" (Jn 10:11-18). As Jesus personifies the light of God's wisdom (Jn 1:4-5), his message (considered foolishness by the world) demonstrates the power of God's wisdom (1 Cor 1:18-25).

Divine wisdom in the words of the Teacher is meant to act as a goad, prodding us to godly action. He also compares it to "firmly embedded nails," reminding us of a godly perspective.

Question 9. Remind your group of how Ecclesiastes was introduced with the statement "Everything is meaningless" (1:2). Now at the conclusion we find the only thing that will prove this wrong—a proper perspective of God and a proper response to him.

Question 10. If it is helpful, point out that the alternative to "fearing God" (12:13; also see 3:17; 5:7 and 8:12) is to fear something less than him—something under the sun. A helpful follow-up question would ask, "What else or who else are you tempted to fear more than God?"

Question 12. Go around the group in order to give each member a chance to respond. End by spending time praying for each person.

Bill and Teresa Syrios live with their boys, Andrew, Phillip, Mark and, sometimes, Luke (now an OSU student) in Eugene, Oregon. Bill operates a real estate investment company, Stewardship Properties. They are also involved with River Oaks Community Church, where Teresa leads the worship team.